Fifty Golden Years

of PATIENCE STRONG

MBW

First published in Great Britain in 1985 by Frederick Muller.

Frederick Muller is an imprint of Muller, Blond & White Limited, 55 Great Ormond Street, London WC1N 3HZ.

British Library Cataloguing in Publication Data

Strong, Patience
    Fifty golden years : a celebration of fifty
    golden years.
    I. Title
    821'.912   PR6037.T847

ISBN 0 584 11131 2
Set by Woodcote Publications Limited, Epsom, Surrey
Printed and bound in Great Britain by
Anchor Brendon Ltd, Tiptree, Essex

Introduction

August 20th, 1935 marked a very special occasion: the first poem by Patience Strong was published in the *Daily Mirror*. Fifty years on, to celebrate her Golden Anniversary as a poet, this Collection has been made from the more than fifteen thousand poems she has had published. *Patience Strong's "Quiet Corner"* appeared regularly first in the *Daily Mirror* and then its sister newspaper *The Sunday Pictorial* later called the *Sunday Mirror.* Her poems continue to appear each week, as they have done for over thirty years, in *Woman's Own* and her message has reached millions across the world.

"May I say 'Thank you' for all the lovely little bits in the *Daily Mirror* each day which you write: they are most beautiful and refreshing and give much food for thought," wrote a reader in 1935 — and her post-bag is still as full as ever.

Patience Strong as early as 1936 wrote movingly of the source of her inspiration: "I have made a very simple, but very important discovery. It's this . . . that if you are relying solely upon material things for your happiness you are bound to be disappointed . . . Unless you find peace and satisfaction within your own soul, you will always be haunted by a sense of frustration, which will act on your nerves and tend to tear down the sources of your body."

Here are twenty-five poems from the last half century — they span the past and the present — years of war and peace, sorrow and gladness, despair and hope. They tell much of the spirit that has sustained our nation through such a varied epoch.

Patience Strong has become a British institution. Consistent, uncompromising and creative she has produced a body of inspirational poetry that has meant so much to so many. As publishers we are glad to present this selection of her most enduring poems.

If You Stand Very Still

If you stand very still in the heart of a wood — you will hear many wonderful things — the snap of a twig, the wind in the trees and the whirr of invisible wings.

If you stand very still in the turmoil of life and you wait for the voice from within — You'll be led down the quiet ways of wisdom and peace in a mad world of chaos and din.

If you stand very still and you hold to your faith you will get all the help that you ask. You will draw from the silence the things that you need: hope and courage and strength for your task.

This little verse established itself by being sent from one country to another enclosed with letters, finding a home at last in a chapel in the redwoods of California where it was recorded, as it happened to be the very thing the builders of the chapel had been hoping to find. Visitors to the chapel in the woods can now hear this record at the press of a button.

Time

Life's a gamble—Life's a scramble—Fret and turmoil—strife and noise; Life's a worry—what's the hurry?—Give me peace and quiet joys.

Life's all clamour—fake and glamour—tinsel shams and vulgar show—Fight for money—aren't folks funny? —rushing madly to and fro.

Give me leisure—simple pleasure—time in which to stand and stare; time to wonder—time to wander—time to dream, and time to spare. . . Time for gazing—time for raising—weary eyes to leaf and wing—time for praying—time for saying—Thank You God for everything.

China Shepherdess

Shepherd boy and shepherdess—two lovers hand in
hand—in the china cabinet—imprisoned there they
stand... Tell me, pretty shepherdess how did you come to
stray—into this grey and grim old town—You should be far
away—in sylvan glades—your dancing feet among the
starry flowers—with your laughing shepherd boy in green
and sunny bowers... Do you dream of verdant vales? and
when the house is still—do you hear the magic flutes that
play upon the hill? Do you tend your snowy flocks beside
the silver streams?—You who have so many hours for long
and quiet dreams... Wait, my pretty shepherdess, you'll be
set free some day—when the people of this town have all but
passed away—the Fairy Folk will come again and down this
silent street—you will hear the patter of a thousand tiny
feet—Mortal hands have locked you in—but wait, and you
shall see—All the Little People will return to set you free...
Wait a thousand years or so of lonely days and nights—You
will feed your flocks again upon the radiant heights—when
this long-deserted town with flowers is overgrown—you
and your good shepherd boy will come into your own...
Following the magic flutes in that enchanted hour—
Making of this grey old town—a green Arcadian bower.

Pamela Jane

Kingdoms could crumble and Empires could crash—Queens could have measles—and banks could go smash—Some great dictator might fall down a drain. But that wouldn't matter to Pamela Jane.

Meddlesome Bishops have altered our prayers (You know the way that they give themselves airs). . . Hitler is doing the goose-step again. But that doesn't matter to Pamela Jane.

Rome is victorious—it's easy to kill—not quite so simple to settle the bill! There's a most horrible rumpus in Spain. But that doesn't matter to Pamela Jane.

Who is this person—this Pamela Jane?—Who is the lady? I wish you'd explain. Pamela Jane thinks that life is such fun—lying all day in her pram in the sun; kicking and gurgling, her wee fingers curled—What should she care for the crazy old world!

The Puddle

The puddle said "I'm good for nothing—In the road I lie—Just a puddle—Such a silly name! What use am I? Wish I'd fallen in a pond, a river or a sea—one bright burst of sun, and there'll be nothing left of me."

A thirsty thrush went flitting through the branches overhead—spied the puddle—"Goodness!—What a bit of luck," he said; swooping down, he took a drink—the best he'd had for days; satisfied—upon the bough—he sang a song of praise.

Someone passing down the street looked up and heard the note—heard the golden fluting of that little feathered throat—One in whom all joy had died and faith had flickered out—one whose spirit wrestled in an agony of doubt. . . Thrilled, he stood and listened to the rapture of that thrush—Lifting up his weary eyes, he saw the sunset's flush—Saw against the flaming sky a cross upon a spire. . . Deep within his heart there stirred an infinite desire—to live, with courage and believe—to rise and dream again—building up his shattered life in spite of grief and pain: knowing God had spoken to him in the twilight hush—Spoken in the sweet untutored language of a thrush. Through that puddle in the road—a soul was born anew. . . So, if there is any little thing that you should do—Do it now—your act may have profound significance—Linking things together, in the chain of circumstance.

Life Is For Living

Life is for living so live it and see—what a thrilling and wonderful world it can be—when you let go of the things that annoy—and start to discover the secret of joy; life is too good to be squandered, too brief—to waste upon grievances, grudges and grief.

Life is for giving, so give of your best. Keep nothing back and your days will be blessed. . . Give time and give money, give thanks and give praise—It will return in mysterious ways. Life was not meant to depress or destroy. Life is for giving and giving is joy.

Be Good To My Girl

Be good to my girl. That's all I ask. She now belongs to
you... Be kind to my lass. Take care of her, for I still love
her too... My daughter always, yes, I know. My daughter,
but your wife. I knew she'd have to go some day, I don't
complain. That's life.

The only thing that matters is that she is going to be...
loved and happy. That is all that really counts with me... So
upon this day of days when hearts are in a whirl—I want to
say just this once more; be good to her, my girl.

Mother To Daughter

I give you to the man you love upon your wedding day. No tear of mine must mar your joy. I send you on your way—grateful for the golden years when you belonged to me—treasuring within my heart each precious memory.

I'm losing you, my dear—but I am more than glad to know—that you have found your love—as I found mine long, long ago . . . And so goodbye, my little girl—God keep you and God bless—granting you life's sweetest blessings, health and happiness.

Guess Who?

At everybody's beck and call, on duty night and day—working. Keeping going in an uncomplaining way—yet with time to stop for you and say a word of cheer... Never coming out on strike, but non-stop year by year—doing this and doing that with quick and willing hands—running to perform with joy whatever love demands.

Is there such a person? Guess. It's Mother, sure enough—on the treadmill of the home. For her the going's tough—but I wonder why it is she always seems to be—the healthiest and happiest member of the family.

Give Me A Quiet Corner

Give me a quiet corner and a little time to hear—the singing of the birds from dawn to dusk throughout the year... Give me a chance to think things out before it's time to go—Give me a place where I can sit and see the sunset glow.

Give me a window with a view that flows to meet the sky. Give me a garden where the trees can feel the winds blow by... Give me good days and sleep-blessed nights when I have closed the door—and anyone can have the world. I'll never ask for more.

Partners

The first dance of all when they danced heart to heart—they
knew, they both knew, it was only the start—of something
more wonderful than a mere dance—more than the thrill of
a passing romance.

They knew without saying that Love, the real thing—had
touched them that night with its shimmering wing. No word
had been spoken and yet they both knew—that suddenly all
sorts of dreams had come true.

It's many a year since the night that they met—but that
first dance they will never forget... Then boy and girl and
now husband and wife—still happy, still dancing, and
partners for life.

Marriage Is Making A Dream Come True

Marriage is sharing with smiles and tears
... whatever may come
with the changing years...
Marriage is learning what life can be—
when two hearts beat in harmony.

Marriage is building from day to day—a
home that's a place where
you both can stay—
happy together, contented there—
whether the weather be foul or fair.

Marriage is loving, unfailingly.
Marriage is kindness and loyalty...
Marriage is making a dream come true—
and keeping the dream ever bright and new.

Walking On A Winter's Day

The crunch of ice beneath your tread. The leafless branches overhead. A wayside cottage thatched with snow...The hedge with hips and haws aglow—becomes a strange and lovely sight—in the bright and frosty light.

Along the lanes you know so well—beauty casts a magic spell. There's much to see and much to learn. At every gate and every turn—you see what summer's green concealed: the distant spire, the far-off field. For when the trees stand stripped and bare—they open windows everywhere...A different landscape you survey—walking on a winter's day.

This Is Christmastide

An island of peace in a sea of turmoil.
This is Christmastide.
A vision of light in a world of shadows.
This is Christmastide.
The promise of something that lies beyond
The torment and the tears.
The glory of God like the rising sun
Across the long dark years.
An echo of music that seems to come
From angels hovering.
The wonderful confirmation of
A strange and lovely thing.
A message that sets all earth and heaven
Ringing far and wide,
The marvellous message that he is with us.
This is Christmastide.

This Be Their Epitaph May 1945

From the clean hands of the young we take the gift supreme: the gift of life and liberty, the right to work and dream... We take what they have won for us, a thing above all price. What do we offer in return for that high sacrifice?

These have served their generation, wise beyond their years—following the flag of faith through mud and blood and tears... We shall remember, though once more we learn to live and laugh. They were the saviours of the world... This be their epitaph.

When I Remember You

I remember a thousand things when I remember you: the firelight glowing on polished oak; a table set for two...The gleam of lamps in a rain-washed street; the shimmer of wet leaves. The smoky grey of November nights. The blue of April eves.

A meeting under a station clock. A song, a smile, a dance. The muted sweetness of violins: the music of romance...A country walk and a cottage tea; a window with a view. I remember a thousand things when I remember you.

To A Newborn Baby

Just a bundle in a shawl, a new-born baby
pink and small.
You're a little miracle—something very
wonderful.
You, a weak and helpless mite, have
emerged into the light,
and arrived upon the earth through
the secret gates of birth.
In your presence I feel shy, and I feel I'd like
to cry.
You're a mystery to me, straight from
Heaven you seem to be.
I stand before you wondering, what the
coming years will bring—
and pray that God preserving you, will keep
you ever pure and true.

To An Adopted Child

We did not bring you into the world—'twas not our destiny—but we chose you for ourselves, our own dear child to be—Our name to bear, our lives to share, a blessing from above—to be the darling of our hearts, to cherish and to love.

Someday you will know the truth. The story we must tell—but I pray you'll understand and love us just as well...God be good and make us wise with strength to carry through—our hopes, our dreams and all the lovely things we plan for you.

Snowdrops

Snowdrops come back every year,
The same yet ever new.
It always thrills you when the first
Green points come thrusting through.
But do you see them as the working
Of a miracle—
Proof of One who loves the world
And makes it beautiful?
Things divine are shown to us,
In little ways expressed,
Messages from realms of spirit,
Hope made manifest.

But That Was Yesterday

The outlook was a gloomy one,
And I had lost my way.
I saw no hope, no sign, no sun,
But that was yesterday.

The Eye Of Faith

The eye of Faith can always see the gold beyond the grey—though the gleam be distant and the glory far away... The eye of Doubt with vision blurred looks out into the night—and sees no promise of the dawn, no glimmering of light.

The eye of Faith can pierce the gloom of grief and tragedy—and through the shadows can behold God's boundless charity.

Cricket

The finest game...the best of all. But it is more than that. More than just a game that's played with wicket, ball and bat...Cricket has become a symbol in the world to-day—of the code of sportsmanship, of fairness and clean play.

The Eton fields, the pitch at Lord's, the park, the village green. Dear unto the English heart is the familiar scene. Ragged boy or white-clad figure with a famous name—playing for the pleasure and the glory of the game.

April Day

Many an exile far away is thinking of an English lane. Many a homesick heart to-day remembers with a stab of pain—Blackthorn wet with April rain; a row of elms; the sound of rooks. Primrose banks and hazel hedges; violets by the wayside brooks.

Down the path of Memory the dreamer wanders and he sees—daffodils in cottage gardens; blossom on the lilac trees... England beckons to her children—calls them home from far away, when her lanes are at their fairest on a lovely April day.

Pictures In The Fire

What do you see in the fire tonight?
I see the oddest things:
A castle on a mountain-top
A bird with flaming wings.
An old old man, a gnome I think.
A dwarf with pointed beard.
A cottage with three chimney pots.
A forest, wild and weird.

I see a ruby-studded cave,
With crimson stalactites.
And just behind that bit of coal
There are the strangest sights.
A lady with a basket
And a small boy with a dog.
Can't you see them seated there
Upon the apple log?

Constance Camellia

She used to come here every night.
By candlelight, by candlelight.
A Shadow-Lady on the wall.
She wore a bonnet and a shawl.
I often wondered how she came
To have so beautiful a name:
    Constance Camellia

Sometimes she stood very still.
But when the wind swooped down the hill
And blew the thin flame to and fro
The Shadow-Lady curtsied low.
Then rising, flounced her wide skirts out
And twirled and swirled and whirled about
Until the wind had ceased to roar
Against the window and the door.
And then quite still she would remain.
A Shadow-Lady once again.

But now, she does not come at all
To spread her skirts upon my wall.
It's only in a dream at night
That she returns by candlelight
And dances with the dancing flame
The lady with the lovely name:
    Constance Camellia

The Healing Years

Though all must suffer loss and grief,
Time is kind and brings relief.
The passing of the healing years
Deadens pain and dries the tears.

At first, hearts break and sorrow numbs,
No word consoles, no comfort comes,
But slowly to the quiet mind
Life flows back, for time is kind.

Tear on the Page

When the Angel of Death in his Book records—the life of some innocent child...I think he must weep as he writes the names of the young and the undefiled.

I think that a tear on the page must fall—though a new soul in Heaven is born—A tear not for those who are safe with God, but for those who are left to mourn.

In Memoriam

Dear was he, a husband, a companion and a friend. Worst and best we faced together, sharing to the end...Plans we made but though our dreams have ended now in tears—I can still be thankful for the blessings of the years.

He has gone beyond my sight a few short steps ahead—going on before me by the road that all must tread...He has gone but love lives on and memories remain—to treasure in my heart until God grant we meet again.